POEM ON DEATH AND DYING

Bahareh Amidi

Death and Dying

adoraarts

Bahareh

cover and interior illustrations by
Adora:
 @AdoraArts

email: connect@bahareh.com
facebook.com/Bahareh.Amidi
twitter.com/BaharehAmidi
youtube.com/baharehLIVE
instagram.com/bahareh_poetess
www.bahareh.com

"I came like water, and like wind I go."
                    - Omar Khayyam

Listen to Poem on Death and Dying

To write about death,
one must first define deat
Is death simply
when we stop breathing
or is it in fact
when we stop living

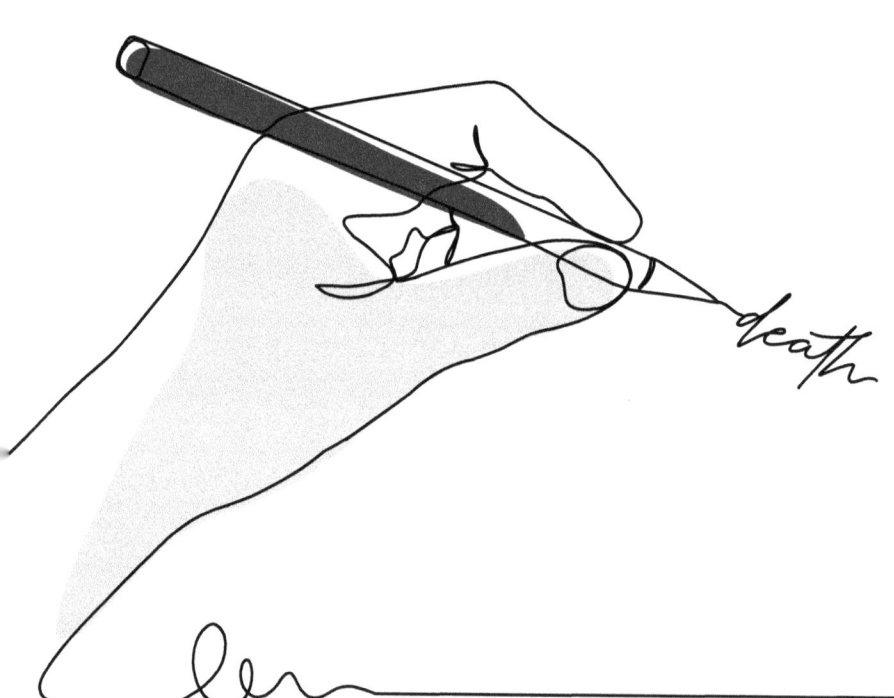

death

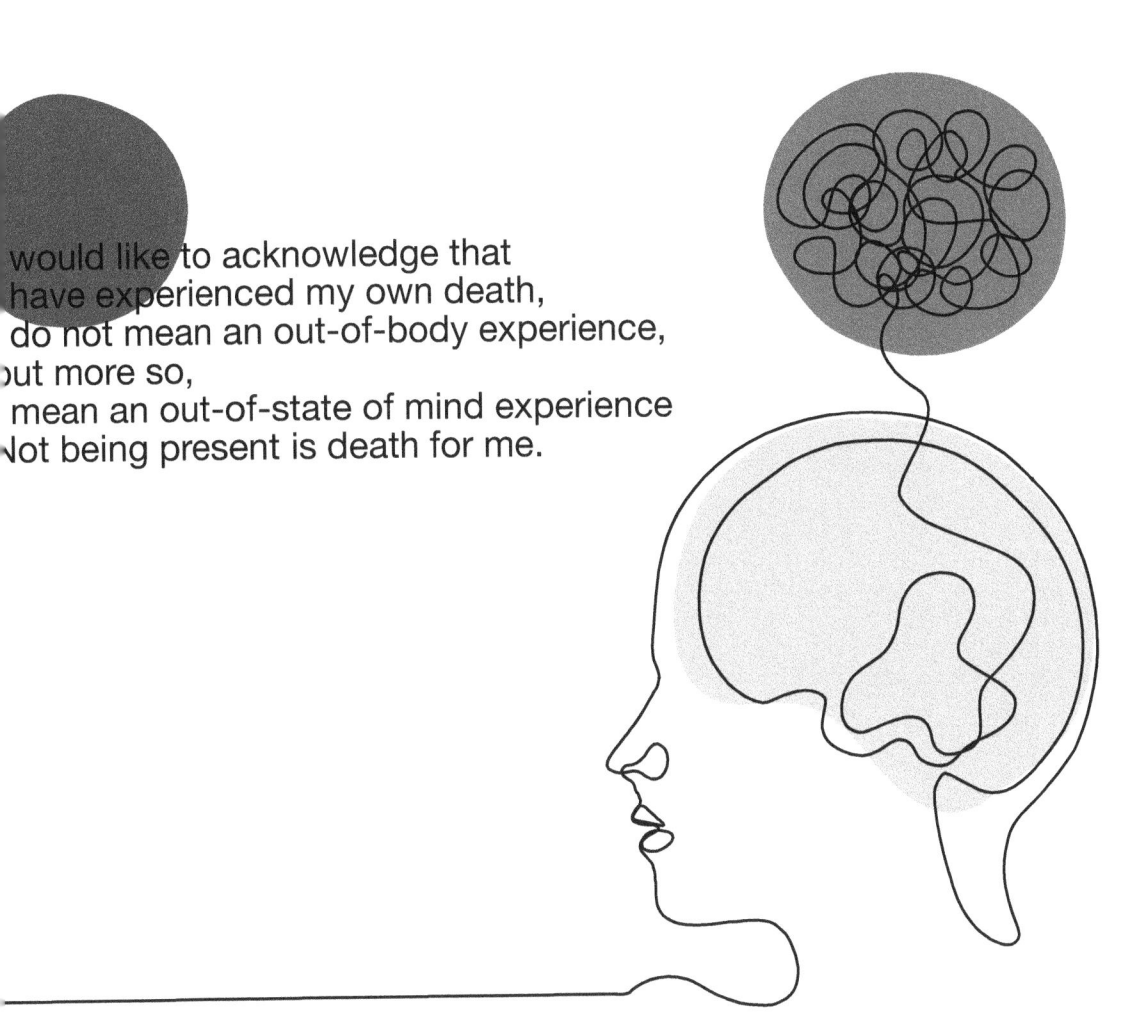

would like to acknowledge that
have experienced my own death,
do not mean an out-of-body experience,
but more so,
mean an out-of-state of mind experience
Not being present is death for me.

I have died,
and I have been born,
not only 44 years ago,
but time after time
with each sunset whose fire
puts ablaze each and every strand of hair
on each and every creature in the sea.

Death from the eyes of the person who is dying
Since the moment I came to this world,
I knew there had to be a time that I would go.
For some around me,
this has been a slow death,
one breath by one breath
as each cigarette was lit
and each ash was dropped to the ground.

For others
it has been a long death of being alone
without a soul to call upon
on their death-bed and to their side
when it is time for washing the body
of its sins to put into the ground.
There is the sudden death,
in a car accident,
or just a call,
as if one's time had come
and one had to answer the call.
A heart attack,
a stroke
and no good byes.

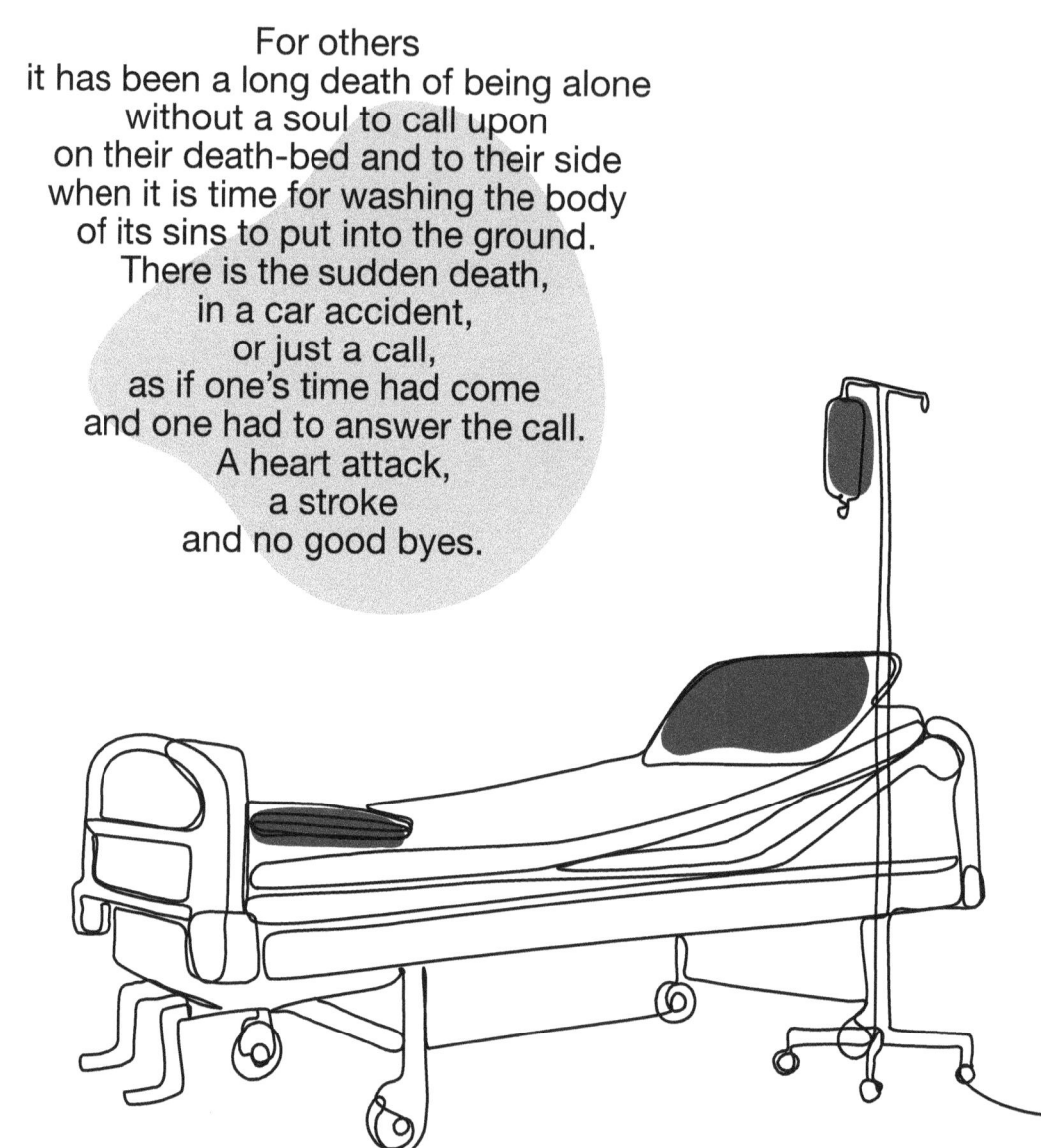

This may be the hardest
for those around,
but indeed
it is the easiest way out
of the cage and into flight.

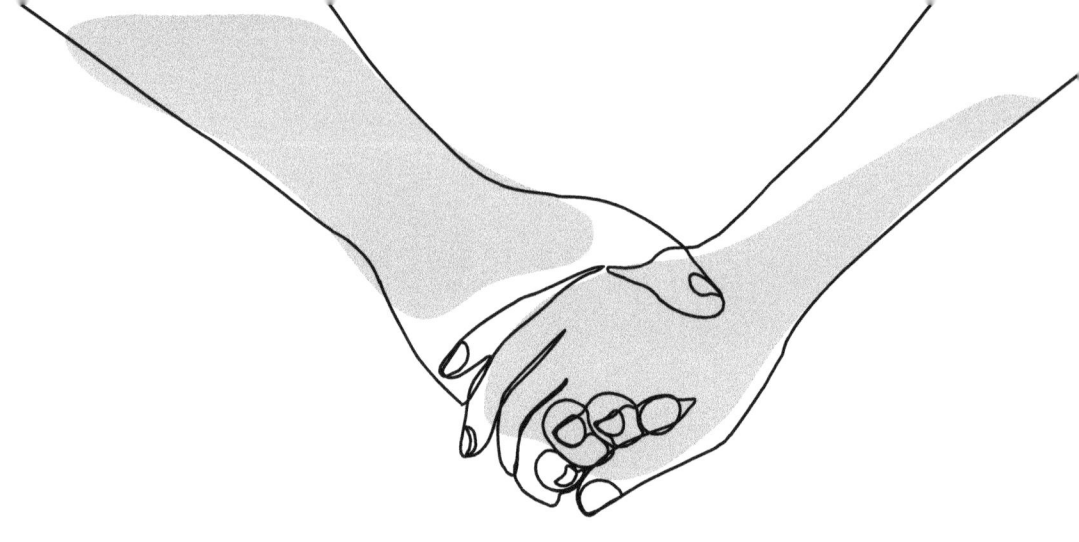

So as the dying person
might think or want to say to those around,
please do not hold on
to my being for I am ready for flight.
Sit with me, but do not hold me.
Hold my hand,
but do not try to hold the life
that is ready to depart.
Just sit with me.
Can you just sit with me.
Thank you

**Death from the eyes of the person
who is sitting next to the dying**
Why are you going so early,
it is not time yet.
But I guess it is never time,
you have suffered long days and nights
and i should be happy for your flight.

I ask you one thing and only one thi
please come to my dream once
and tell me of your where abouts.
I guess I want to know
where I am heading.
Is it as peaceful as they say,
or is it as hot in hell
as is depicted in the holy books.
I will remain next to you,
do not fear,
I will miss you,
but I will release you.

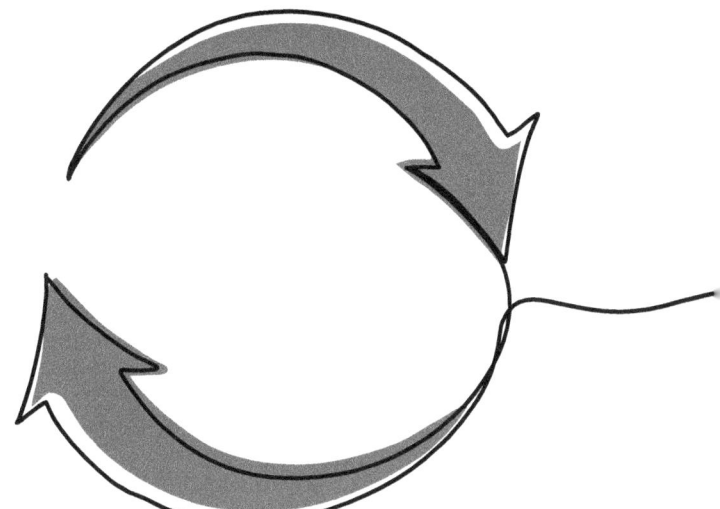

Death from point of view of the Universe

knew 22 years ago,
when you were born that today was the day of return
knew 44 years ago,
when you were born that today was the day of return
knew 88 years ago,
when you were born that today was the day of return
Ashes to ashes dust to dust.
With each birth the cycle flows
and with each death the cycle continues to flow.
The ebb and flow of the beauty of life and death.

In speaking of life and death,
it is not as if I have forgotten
about suicide and homicide,
but indeed,
I have not much to say about taking a life,
may it be your own or other's lives.
I would just say,
I hope in such a state,
may a person just stop for a minute
and consider a grin on a child's face
or a wrinkle on an old man's face
and then take a breath
and take another breath
and know that the next one after
that is a gift and nothing but a gift.